LEAVES SURFACE LIKE SKIN

Also by Michelle Menting

Residence Time (chapbook)
Myth of Solitude (chapbook)

LEAVES SURFACE LIKE SKIN

by

Michelle Menting

Terrapin Books

Terrapin Books
4 Midvale Avenue
West Caldwell, NJ 07006

www.terrapinbooks.com

ISBN: 978-0-9982159-1-4
LCCN: 2017940739

First Edition

Cover Art by Christine J. Higgins
Cover Design by D. Robert Johnson

For my siblings,
and in memory of my mother

Contents

*The leaves of memory seemed to make a mournful rustling
in the dark.*
—Henry Wadsworth Longfellow

*There is something infinitely healing in the repeated
refrains of nature—the assurance that dawn comes after night,
and spring after winter.*
—Rachel Carson

The snow is melting into music.
—John Muir

I

To Skin Bare

The lichen sticks to bark grooves like skin, but dead,
dried, and peeling. Like damaged skin. Diseased skin.

It's skin of another, and there's a strangeness
in the act of stripping it. Almost shy. Almost

aware of some kind of compelled intrusion. Wayward
intimacy. Compulsion to intrude right there

on a log of balsam. You peel. You strip. You take off
the skin of this other thing. Imagine it's like peeling scabs,

not yours, a friend's, a stranger's. Or taking off clothes,
not yours, a stranger's. You can think these things in the woods.

In the woods, if you have a thought and then another
and another thought, but no one is there to watch you

weather your notions as you strip lichen off bark, as you peel
bark from tree, as you reveal the bare trunk and the ooze of sap,

does anyone sense your thought-quake? If anything
is moved—if anything shudders, if anything shakes—

it is only your own unheard heart, its wavering
wick, the dormant layers it beats beneath.

Upon Encountering in the Woods the House with No Driveway, No Trail, No Footpath Leading to the Front Door

Lights on, and they appear as a false sunset through
the forest wall. Their glow tricks, says, *Here is clearing.*
Space. Open. Free. Walk here. Like a lone Gretel, you do.
This house has vents like lungs that parcel the air, parse dust
in two: outside blow bits of leaves and pollen; inside, cat hair,
shit from mites, scales from a garter's shed. The siding flakes
in gaudy eyelashes, the sort you imagine on vaudeville clowns
(who welcome with menace, with grins in union with grimace).
This house is surrounded, circled by spruce and firs that peer
into windows. Their needles collect in the corners of the frames.
These trees don't practice personal space. They claw and scratch
the siding, each other. They reach and grasp the needles they've lost.
Or do they lament the wooden strips, curled with rot, that once
were branches, their cove of relatives' bark? This house,
it troubles: the breeze, the trees, and the people. There are people.
Are there people? Rocking inside, rocking in chairs, rocking
in place on a loveseat couch with bended frame and houndstooth
fabric. Cats, phantoms of black, on hollowed laps. So bare,
everything so worn, everyone so thin. So see-through.
Could these cats be shadows? Could these people wisp through
the lungs of vents, out the cracks in the window panes?
Would their forms drift outside into the limbs of spruce and fir
in a waltz of bough and breath? Would pine needles pierce any skin?

What We Know about Deer Season

We know about urine, how our scent deflects
bucks and does, and so we know to crouch, to let
the gold streams loose within sight of deer stand scopes.
We know to do this early, like spies who protest,
before the shooting begins.

We remember to scarf Sonny, to twist
his Labrador hair with saffron bows.
We know to always, always walk him leashed,
to wear construction vests, pumpkin-colored gloves,
hats dyed tangerine, and to whistle while we walk.

We've seen the roadways covered with men
driving from Chicago, from Milwaukee,
even Topeka. We know about dollar deals
on Pabst Blue Ribbon, about Free Salt Blocks!
with every Kessler-by-the-case purchase.

We know about titty bars, the peroxided strippers
prepared for the hunters' hostel, and shooter shows
under the pines. We know it's tradition.
We know they say it is.

We know school will be sparse this week. Students
with parents like ours, like us, the only kids there.
We know we'll play twister, touch bodies, flirt
with the Reddy boys, who play hockey and are Hindu.
We know there'll be extra cheese in the cafeteria.

We know to avert our eyes as we make our way
through the parking lots into grocery stores.
We know about flatbed trucks, the not-yet fawns
with their acorn prongs and their bellies sliced open.

Displacement Activity of Our Neighbor Who Was Once a Taxidermist (or a Serial Killer)

Instead, he paints pictures of animal deaths: the suicides
birds perform in the yard, or the bat with its belly pulsed
and inflated (its corpse, so tiny, the muscles turned tender
on the driveway's concrete: still wet, still lending some stick).
He buries dead bunnies drowned in the storm, their bodies
turned hairballs: sodden and twisted in the wet cut grass.
He snaps their pictures before placing them all
in a morgue of shoeboxes. Then he stretches their images
to hundreds of pixels by painting with acrylics
all the smudged reds, the feathered blacks, the yellows
lacking good humor. The canvas becomes bumped,
resurfaced with mounds of paw and specks of beak,
strokes of tail. Once the dead of the yard now possessed
indoors up on his mantel. Caged in frame as lasting art.

Of Your Brother, Who Left for the War Today

I haven't met him, not yet, not soon,
but you showed me that picture,

the two of you in the mountains, the rocks
in the background all cragged like a snapshot

of a shudder as if chills could be caught
on the face of stones. If only you with your gaze,

that half-sober smile—drunk from nostalgia
and bonding over beers—could buffer that landscape,

could blanket those sharp edges, place everything
in soft focus. But the focal point, the real one

if I could pick it, was that pale yellow flower,
the one your brother grazed with his left index finger.

Its stem, bent and leaning, bowed across the space
between the two of you. In the background,

just a glimpse of sky. And all those rocks and boulders
stuck in that photograph, with you with your brother,

will remain in that western land, will be there in autumn
when we drive out to watch the prairie grass copper,

when we look out across the crevices of rock,
when we climb the foothills and wait.

On the First Day of Class, We Wrestle Heuristics

What was your first nickname? Did it include
your first pet (*Mittens*) and the road (*Shady Lane*)
you lived on when you were ten?
(Did children make fun of your stutter
or lisp? Did they call you *Mitten-Spittens*,
Thady Thlane, Shady Spit-Shit?)

What are your two truths, your one lie?
(Is the lie more interesting? Your truth
a lie you convinced yourself is true?)

Your favorite food—what is it? Would you eat
roadkill for $1000 (for friendship or love)?

Have you traveled somewhere warm
when you lived somewhere cold?
(Was the warmth outside, the cold
in your heart?)

How many siblings do you have (do you wish
you had fewer, like after Thanksgiving
when your stomach is full, your mouth
empty of words and dry of spite)?

Your favorite activity—what is it? Do you run,
draw, ski, dance (spy, wait for the mail carriers
just to ask them about their shoes)?

What scares you, really scares you?
Does this scare anyone else?
(Would you be less afraid if it did?)

What would your superpower be? To fly,
to heal, to disappear (to reappear in yesterday,
last week, last year)? (Were you born too late?
Too soon? Born again?)

If you could be someone else, anyone at all, anyone
other than you, who would you be?
(Who are you? Will you tell us who you are?)

Upon Learning about Tardigrades from Wikipedia

*Tardigrades are tiny, water-dwelling animals originally
named kleiner Wasserbär, meaning "little water bear" in
German. In Italian, tardigrada means "slow walker." The
name water bear comes from the way they walk, reminiscent
of a bear's slow gait.*

If we ate by sucking, preying on juice of moss, skin shake
of algae; if we pierced cell walls with our stylets—with foregut,
hindgut, everything embraced, bringing new meaning to feeling
with your gut, going by your gut, gut as instinct; if we could hug
the litter of lichen, cling to swamp lily petals, take a free ride
from the gills of mussels, as if sitting in our own airstream trailers;
if we experienced ourselves as ourselves: dining on parasites
while being parasitic. What if we were nothing more than layers
of dust with heartbeats? It's true: the idea of invisibility
can make my own skin crawl, but they float, their lives aquatic,
they float. Blow them up. Take micro to macro and see their forms
with rolls: *water bear, moss piglet, puddle manatee.* Almost jolly.
But they suck. They cannibalize. They go for the extreme: once
they were found on heaps of dung balls on glaciers, on frozen clumps
of vegetal innards. Everywhere, everywhere absorbing. Absorbing
the universe in millions upon millions of eight tiny segments.
Let's find them. Find them to better understand the guts of the bizarre.

Jill Falls for Jack

Really, they fell from bramble-scrawled oak trees,
became snow angels without snow. Instead
they made wings from the swept scars of lawn grass.
After the mower blade cut, they tucked
green shards between armpits, against elbows.
It was still summer, but hardly, and they took turns
jumping off limbs to let the wind escape them, again
and again. On purpose they fell. Their throats scratched
as they gasped for air, first he, then she. And then he
reached over, put his lips on hers and blew breath,
mouth to mouth, as if she suffered from drowning,
as if her lungs were pails of water instead of dry,
hollow. Until she breathed in, and the wind again
made her feel like tumbling, like tumbling after.

Smarch

Last year, we changed the name,
first called it shit-March, then Smarch:
a month of foreboding weather.
What was there to look forward to?
Gray snow, backyards full of dog shit,
spring break with no money and nowhere
to go? Here, spring is all wrong,
where the lake dominates and flannel
becomes second skin by May. And everyone
wants escape from heat as forced air, forced
courtesy, forced conversation. We're no different.
That scare we had on the Ides, in the car,
the deer outside skittering black ice,
our brakes on the same surface? That moment
of flashed cliché—I saw you, you saw me,
and we were parting beyond possibilities
of crunched metal, busted spleens—
should have served as soothsaying.
But no. Instead, just like the month itself,
there we sat weeks later with February's
leftovers: crushed valentines still stuck
and abandoned in mailboxes, the melting snow,
with more brewing on the lake's horizon.
Toward our end, when finally it came
like crocuses sprouting, we still strapped on
boots and smiles as morning routine. We still
grabbed our tools as we headed out the door,
for you the shovel, for me the salt.
We cleared the front walk.
We made it safe to pass on by.

Sky Writing

To shuffle boots in snow, link letters
with feet. Write frosted notes for the above,
readable only while high in flight.
Years ago, when I was pre-tween I wrote
on lake ice, scooted Sorels from letter
to letter, below a cloudless winter sky.
I wrote, HI UP THERE and HELP, THE FISH
ARE FROZEN or LAND HERE and I ♥ BOBBY,
the boy with the curls. My audience
was birds—bewildered chickadees,
lost geese, late ducks lounging
out past the holidays, and jets
that circled and screeched, wrote back
in return just loops of foreign cursive—doodles
frozen fish could not answer.
But that 10-year-old girl, rural and quiet,
thought: there, finally, contact.

II

Front Porch, Summer 1993

After   her breakup

      my older sister   explains

the perils of passion:

See   that firefly

      flash   the pavement?

Watch   as I squash it

            beneath

                  my bare foot.

To Fell Roaches

Cockroaches Respond to Peer Pressure, Study Suggests
—The New York Times, 2007

In nuclear fallout films, like the ones my brothers watched
on Sunday afternoons between the Packers and the Vikings
on our only channel with clear pictures, cockroaches ruled.
It didn't matter that the heroine had big breasts, enough fat
to handle the starved weeks ahead, or that the hero was crafty
with pipe bombs and wheat germ. Even if the couple
and the orphaned 5th-grader, a tagalong with his stray dog
blue heeler (cleverly named Blue), escaped the zombies
and the leather-clad neo-Nazis, the bugs would get them
in the end. In apocalyptic films, insects always inherit the earth.
If only the hero (the war vet who lost everything) or the heroine
(rail thin with two exceptions) or that scrappy kid with the 180 IQ,
or even Dog Blue knew about peer pressure and how to engage
a single cockroach in a game of Truth or Dare. Then, like lemmings
running over the edge, all those roaches would have fallen.

What We Salvaged

from the barn after the fire, the smoke, the wreckage,
was nothing we'd hoped to save: crisp halters, blackened
bridle bits, charred maple oat bins, lead lines of nylon
melted to shoelace width, and smoldering slats
of wood once lofted for hay now damned to the floor,
stewed with dirt, damp straw, and manure.

Somewhere in the back was the worst of it all, most of them
intact but contorted, as if they'd huddled in the corner
for comfort. Or worse. What if they pushed their bodies
against the barn's door, prayed in their way, that the latch
would burst, the gate would open, and their new home
forever would be meadows of May, their roof the 2AM sky?

We heard nothing that night. The dogs paced, for sure,
but it was spring and the woods always call in that pitch
only dogs can hear. How many times have I envied
the ears of hounds, to be able to listen for bobcat rustling
a quarter mile away? That night before bed, we brewed
bags of chamomile, put bagels in the toaster so we could sleep

more evenly, dream more sound. Now every time a teakettle
steams—whinnies before shrieking—I smash my palms
against my ears. I try to overcome that pitch of smoke.

On Learning It's the Midwestern Weather That Makes Us All Crazy

Maybe atmospheric pressure
　　　　discombobulates us.
Or maybe the rain breaks
　　　　into maple syrup, runny
instead of downpour,
　　　　and all the weathermen
become pancakes, soak in sticky sweetness,
　　　　and tell us all about it.
Maybe we all fall down rabbit holes,
　　　　meet talking cats trapped down
in the tunnel to China. The tabbies get stuck
　　　　somewhere beneath the Bering Strait—
eat too many shrimp to waddle back up
　　　　manholes in Chicago.
Maybe pigs ride bicycles and dreams
　　　　birth baby zebras from the tops of our heads.
And what does drunkenness do? Makes us balance
　　　　our checkbooks? And drugs—hardcore,
inject-in-the-arm narcotics?
　　　　Do the needles and inhalants
warm us up for coffee and delightful conversation
　　　　at Starbucks? We then mow the lawn,
take out the trash? We go shopping
　　　　for kitchen appliances. We do the usual.
We drive our car to the pedestrian mall.
　　　　We don't even pray
we don't get shot looking at shoes.
　　　　We don't even notice
pigs on Schwinns, or how everything
　　　　sticks to umbrellas.

First Snow Aubade

Now suncups pock the feeder, and the birds scratch seeds
from flakes. Last night, we thought we heard a loon lost
in the middle of November. How it must have fallen out of August
and spent the months of autumn concussed to finally wake
in this sudden preamble of winter. We were wrong, of course.
In this wind and forest of naked limbs, words are sparse
and the leaves rustle away any sense in our syntax.
This much is true: now is not the partnering time.
The temperature drops outside, and inside the valves of our hearts
solidify as if becoming oak stems: so brittle each pump threatens
to break artery from organ. But this is wrong. We are healthy
but changing and mishear what we say. We want to hear
a loon's tremolo, we want its wail, its calling to a mate.
We want this longing to be real, and the sound so sorrowful,
it would weep the rime from the cattails in the wetlands.
We want, but even the effort of want fails to surprise us
into thawing. At dawn, on my walk to feed the chickadees,
I found two squirrels. Their heads removed. At the stumps
of their necks, were the reddest berries of blood. And beyond
the knotted fingers of forest, a hawk lifted off from the tallest pine.
When its talons released the branch, frost shattered and fell into flakes
that flashed in the opening sun. With each flap of its wings
the sound wavered, created that false tremolo misheard as wailing.
But I was too slow to cover my ears to block out that bird's call, its voice
that speared the morning fog, that severed last breaths from warmth.

Residence Time

Residence time (also called "lake retention time" or "flushing time") refers to the calculated amount of time water spends in a particular lake. It is also the amount of time it takes for a substance, once introduced into the water, to finally flow out of the lake.

My sister tells us the true story
   about when she was hit by a truck.
This isn't a tragedy, she says, *but a flash*
   of true fiction. And she tells us
how she went running, how she took off
   that day hours before dawn, before any of us
pulled back our blankets and stretched.
   Already she'd covered eight miles of back roads
bordered by pine trees before the Chevy Half Ton
   or Ram Jeep Hummer *monster*
of a truck driven by a smaller monster hit her,
   clocked her good, made her spin and kiss the tar.
She recalls the backstory, how once she babysat
   the driver when he was five: how he'd dug
his fingers into the grass, then pulled
   fistfuls of sod and stuffed the sprigs, roots and all,
into his mouth and thumbed his nose
   at the year-round kids who came over for cookies
and Transformers. His coordination
   was all pumps and smacks, even then,
like an overgrown baby who knows manipulation.
   He was cute, she says, waddling
with precision even at five, his legs so accustomed
   to a bellyful of beef and not of poached venison.
That summer in our northern town,
   where everyone knew everyone's golden retrievers,
my sister, back from college, watched the children
   of part-time residents for full-time pay.

Fifteen years later while we sit around the campfire,
    all of us home reuniting near the lake,
she finishes her story with the smack of that truck,
    how it bruised her thigh, how she felt hot air
after her left hip bounced off the blacktop pavement.
    But she kept her head held high, she says,
like when you stretch your neck to keep from drowning.
    She noticed the early sun. She foreshadowed its rising.

The Effigy Mounds

We slipped over the embankment, picked
wildflowers we thought invasive along the way.
On the trail to the mounds, our footfalls echoed,
first one then the other, the crushing of leaves,
the popping of acorns on twigs.
When we reached the clearing, there running freely
atop those ancient hills, were troops of kindergartners,
construction paper in their hands, each page
circled in green and flapping in the wind.
Beneath their feet, were the waves of beasts
and rounds of breasts. *Effigies,* the literature said,
commemorating the past. Loved ones. Sacred.
You tapped my shoulder, nodded towards raised coils
ridging from soil. *Snake,* you said. *Serpent,*
I corrected, and pointed toward a glossy page.
A six-year-old ran by, his picture was a reptile
with legs of a man chasing a bear, its serpentine tongue
reaching, reaching. Your hand cupped my shoulder,
then slid to my breasts—first one then the other.
Breasts, you said, nodding towards twin mounds
surrounded by birch and covered with children.
We sat near the edge on the underside of cleavage—
plant stems poking closer at the slope.
The wind picked up, the kids soon left,
and we sank down, rested against the swells of land.
They're full of charcoal, you know—fuel for heat.
And this seemed right, though I'd thought
they were hollow, just like sculptures: the art exists
only on the outside. We slept right there against
the rise of breasts and placed our ears against their tilt.
We hugged our hands around their crest, felt
for warmth. Lulled in the grass, sacred and breathing.

III

The Day I Lost the Boy to the Girl with Sea-Foam Manners and Wave-Motion Hips

And there was no fairness to any of it. That day, I learned
the saying "life isn't fair" is more than just an incomplete
bumper sticker, and that "all's fair in love and war" means nothing
to the drafted. And by drafted, I mean smitten by surprise.
And by surprise, I mean hormones that miraculously rev up
and function. And by function, I mean take over the heart, the mind,
whatever organ operates reason. And by reason, I mean knowing
the difference between desperation and love. And by love,
I mean the flowerbed daydreams, the ponytail play, the mmmbop
longings of a 12-year-old girl. And by 12-year-old girl,
I mean me, without breasts, without hips, without the ability
or just plain know-how to bat long eyelashes, be coy
and coo like some cartoon sea creature or southern belle—all teasing
politeness and cordial temptation—in movies with boat bow dresses.
And by cordial temptation, I mean the girl with sea-foam manners—
light, flippant—with a name like Tarah with an H or Izabelle
with a Z, who owns her hips, possesses them, controls their curve,
their sway. And by sway, I mean the pulling of the tide, like waves
that capture a soul with rocking. A rhythm like hypnosis.
Or possibly a spell, like the voodoo Tarah with an H or Izabelle
with the wave-motion hips cast on the boy, on me, on anyone
barefoot and walking the shoreline of lapped foam. All of us
enchanted, sent adrift and floating in gales of youth and gloss.

When a Cup of Tea Should Do

*The nervous system is very sensitive to all forms of mercury; its
effects on brain functioning may result in irritability, changes in
vision or hearing, and memory problems.*
    —The Agency for Toxic Substances and Disease Registry

1.

These days on days when you're unsure
of yourself (& so many others), you think
about biting the dictionary. You thought you read
or heard from someone (at some other time)
that ink in print is full of mercury, that mercury
can craze, can blur, can make a person weep
into madness. If you swallowed whole words
soaked in that element—if you absorbed them inside
your insides—would they digest into lunacy?

2.

You didn't cry or wail when you were ten and playing
mad scientist: a thermometer in one hand, a swiped match
in another, and seconds later, a glob of quicksilver
orbed on top the stone kitchen counter. How you loved
the shine of that metallic bead, how it stayed firm
and whole, unbothered by everything, even your fingers
that poked and pressed, tried splicing its luster
into so many pieces. You don't recall what came next,
if you grabbed more thermometers, popped them
for sake of shine. You only think of that silver, that ink,
that toxic metal & match experiment because of something
once read (or heard once read) from someone
(& somewhere) and then only maybe. You think this now
because the dictionary is open to the middle of M
where an imprint of teeth dogears the page.

3.

On that same bookshelf of reference (or fiction?)
you own a copy of *Alice's Adventures*—a gift
from childhood, perhaps your tenth year, a book
with peeled cover and fraying back spine. And with print,
you wonder, if bit, if chewed, you could swallow
somehow-oh-somehow into some kind of madness.

Pharmaceutical

To draw blood from a mouse,
first alcohol the tail. Get it wet
and bare—the liquid does this,
plasters hair to lucid skin.
The tail becomes cordlike
or remnant of cord. It whips,
all three to four inches whip
against your latex glove.
You can do this
one-handed: hold the rodent
down, insert the smallest needle
and extract. Or push. Inject
happiness, clear skin, smooth cuticles,
or erections for 85th birthdays.
With a cage of six, you'll practice.
Wield your syringe like a weapon. Draw
blood, insert saline. Practice
on more. Soon, you'll graduate
to rat gavage, to birth control
for beagles, then learn the P's & Q's
of chromosomal X's & Y's.
You'll get promoted
to lab-coat status
for liquefying immortality.
For encapsulating everlasting love
in tablet form.

Blastomycosis

Blastomyces dermatitidis is endemic to the vicinity of the Great Lakes and is more commonly diagnosed in pets than in humans.

We put the dog to sleep today.

Her lungs now sunken rafts

in the moat of her chest.

But her bones—

now, her bones—

the weight of sparrows.

Ginger's Last Dream

I have seen dead horses, and I am sure they do not suffer pain.
—The horse Ginger in Anna Sewell's *Black Beauty* (1877)

She trips softly as if on purpose. Falls onto married bales
of hay and twine. Her hooves, so wrought with chips,
steel flecks still cling to those ghosts of old shoes.
The clipped paths to her heels are reminders of a farrier
who mouthed the nails before gripping her hocks and shoeing.
He'd let her lean on him, her hip cocked, almost delicate.
Surely that man knew otherwise. Hadn't he heard
the tales of the red filly who galloped through fence hedges,
kicked cart rails pulled by geldings, and expanded her belly
so girls couldn't cinch tight girths on saddles? *The devilish mare.*
But she remembers simply being less tired: those nights in pastures
roaming with Beauty, kicking dew for coolness, playing wild ponies.
She dreams, because all horses do, about the stomping
of meadow grass, those barley-padded echoes under shoeless feet.

Springs Eternal

How hopeful is the northerner
who took pride in her shovel
during long winter snows,

who now grasps the handle, considers
the dull blade, hangs it back
upon rusted nails inside the garage?

In mudrooms, rugs furrowed
with boot liners and mittens
will soon be harvested, then replanted

with umbrellas and galoshes.
Fishing poles with bobbers
will replace tip-ups with flags.

In March, shadows creep from rodents
reborn from burrows. For months
those hedgehogs, muskrats, and beavers

slept drunk underground, underwater,
and knew nothing of wind-chills
and gales past November.

How innocent to wake up hungover
from a party you never did crash.

On Lake Halfsestina

On our northern July night, we loaf. We imitate lichen
and breathe as salamanders do, through our skin.
We're still. We're cautious, for any muscle twitch, any movement,
might turn droplets of sweat—small at first on the surface—
into running rapids, into pools of condensed heat.
When loons call from the lake, their porous sounds liberate the leaves.

We part eyelashes from eyelashes and place our feet on cool leaves
to tiptoe the wooded path. Grasping the trunks of lichen,
we follow the loons' tremolo to take a dip from the heat,
to savor their black water, to let it loosen our skin.
The lake swallows our ankles when we wade its surface.
We laugh. We listen as our echoes mimic the waves' movement.

The clouds, with wisped fingers, shove the buck moon into movement.
My sisters and I look up and watch as the light leaves.
And then? We link arms. We bob like apples at the surface.
We wonder: who out there knows what tranquility feels like?
So we make a pact to merge below. We accept scales for skin.
Diving into wet sleep, we become child-fish: free from breath,
    free from heat.

To Sound Local

I stand outside the co-op with a bottle of beer and a bar
of dark chocolate. This weather slows all heartbeats,
reminds everyone of their premature lust
for spring. I crave it too.

On my side of the store window framing
organic cherries and black mission figs, snow
sweeps the sidewalk, hides beneath
the corners of a bench, the one with looped grillwork
and arms that connect to warped wooden slats.

I know that bench. I used to sit there on Thursdays
in late May when mud made everything smell
like potatoes left in bottom cabinets for far too long
and far past edible. On those days I'd stay and listen
for whistles from freighters coming and going
with shipments of ore.

Singing Gordon Lightfoot was too much a cliché,
but sometimes I'd hum him anyway.
Maybe, I thought, after a while, the organic shoppers
coming and going, matching the traffic of freighters
on the big lake just a block away, would join me
in a verse or two, but no one ever did.

The ships came in and the whistles blew
so close and so often but no one seemed to notice.
I sat every Thursday all of May with my bag
of spring fare: maple syrup, local wine, in-season
asparagus. Sometimes I sat so quietly, so still,

I could listen to all that belonged, to everything
local: the ships on the water blowing their horns,

the voices of other shoppers—all their words
accented with dying y's, the noise of gulls swooping
then scavenging, and the waves of that lake—huge
and swallowing the shore.

Now I stand in temperatures hovering around freezing.
Winter quiet comes from that lake—the shipping season still
months away. There's only wind, a few silent shoppers.
And on that bench, a glaze of ice.

First Single Degree Day Before Winter

Skin on sidewalk ice, skin that's the bottom
halo on window glass, skin on my fingers—
all of it cracking, splitting in patterns of starburst.
Even our collie licks ice melt beneath her paws
then bites a nail and tugs the split tip.
Flurries gather in the nook between the porch
and house. Everything is cold static on the edge
of eruption. This chill is birth of memory, of every
winter's beginning. But too soon. In one gasp,
autumn broke up with us and deprived us
of its orgasm, its season transforming. The trees
and their rusted leaves, any remainder of gold
on grass—all relationships shocked
in the wake of frost. I miss you. I miss it all:
the last warm breath of fall, your long eyelashes
that would capture then bead with fading rain,
our shared Carhartt folding—that jacket you swiped
from your brother's garage—how it swallowed
and devoured your silk-thread frame as you stacked
chopped wood, what we thought would wait
until December to burn. Now on our dog's nose,
a solitary snowflake settles. Stays frozen. Still
hopeful, she does not bother to brush it away.

IV

Waning

Full moon tonight. Careful. Close your drapes. Fondle
your silverware. Resist the urge to howl
and rampage. The day, still bright but lonely, fools
          no one. We all know

about hunger, about want, about cycles—
so many turns of leaves then snow, mud then green
then flower—but the moon, with its craters and glow,
          why does it pull you?

The myths, the lore, the fairytales
(of hairy beasts dressing as grandmas of little girls
in devilish red cloaks) fingertip on true,
          hint at what is real.

But here's what's real: you're no wolf. Moonlight
on lichen, it varies. Shadows slink on trunks
behind you as you make your way towards me
          to meet in secret.

My secrets are just scenes alive in daytime:
my waking laugh at 8AM, chats at noon
with neighbors over tea, tooth-picked olives
          stolen from grocers,

swooped hairstyles, and rain setting the stage
for late-day sun. All this you miss, these fully lighted
affairs. All that's open, public, known
          before any hint of moon.

How, Now from Our Front Doorway You Can See a Fairway

Maybe the moon rises like this everywhere?
Wide, reflecting the pond in the middle

of a golf course? We laughed: *how*
coarse, a course of golf. How now

we went from a home in the woods
to puddle and turf. Now,

we look from a gate with wire
that wraps the remaining pines: how, now

they fence the land. Still, that moon,
once buck now harvest, is slow

but full over the tree line. Low
and looming. Too orange to be safe.

Hunter Orange

A fabric so bright, hops-soaked riflemen
    can smell citrus through their eyelids.
It's like starburst, like cartooned starfish—
    spot-stark under the sea illuminated.
Brilliance like that would shock anyone
    awake from a Miller High Life slumber.
You wouldn't think to point and shoot
    at a walking tangerine. But retriever gold
or labrador yellow so closely resembles
    the hides of bucks and does, and in the woods
in autumn, auburn-haired girls and boys
    better wear scarves woven thick with threads
of sunset. One year in November, when late leaves
    clung to trees and still bled chlorophyll,
I stretched upon a blanket of forest moss and pine.
    Camouflaged and motionless, I sat and listened
to distant shouts of fire—the sounds like rockets, zapped
    cherry bombs after Independence Day parades.
And above, all the colors still sparked the sky.

The Awkward Sister's Complaint

For some, the world is wood tick wicked.
Sloped in spring thaw, the muck of snowmelt
skirts my jeans, and the beaded blood-
suckers creep beyond the pine tree boughs.
Drawn to every puff of your warm breath,
you'd think they smell your skin beneath
your hot pink parka. How I hate that thing
and its many variations: the fall corduroy,
the bubblegum vest, the summer track jacket.
And your hair in its braid, long and swinging,
between your shoulders, stuck in the valley
along your spine, it's so perfect, so straight.
How is it possible to love so much of all
and everything? The perfumed, the flowered,
even the muddy and streaming—spring
for you is looking forward to the plucking
of tulips, the petals you'd use for some recipe
of fawning—some puppy love delight.
But when I sit in a meadow and blow
a blade of grass—when I try to whistle
against its sharp edge—the sound is porcine,
a panicked squealing, and no one and nothing
is summoned to wonder. Only the wood ticks
arrive with curious glee. How great is their luck
that I slice my finger while tuning the stem,
that I leave the blood to dot my lips.

Couch-Surfing Upper Michigan after Lincoln, Nebraska

In the morning there's flannel-knit arm sleeves
       covered in coonhound hair and you almost drink
a carcass of daddy longlegs from someone's coffee cup,
but you don't regret this wake. If you had slept
       on some sofa anywhere else, you wouldn't have met
the guy with the eye-patch worn on his chin, or the girl
who sands decks for fivers a plank. No man named Jameson
       would have inspected your earlobes for nibbles by foxes
(or told you that's what he intended to do), and who
would have listened, entranced and greedy, to your story
       about buffalo dazed on I-80 with that twister approaching?

That story you stole from your student back in Lincoln,
       that student who left one semester in
(but shared with you that very first day: *I grew up in a place
       called Valentine*).

She wrote, months later and from somewhere else, to confess
       her words were all a sham, everything said
in her essay On Experience: there were no buffalo ramming her car,
       or tornado turning rows of corn,
and that town of Valentine?—it exists somewhere,
       but you weren't disappointed when you found out
she never lived there. Only once did she visit a friend of a friend,
       stayed on a couch and listened to stories about some crazy
far and away from anything Nebraska: *did you hear the one
       about that guy, how he dressed as a pirate, long past Halloween,
       after wandering out drunk in the woods one night?*
How he got lost in the dark, woke the next day, earless, in a den full of foxes?

Backwoods Colloquial

You say *hine-jez*, as in "take the door
off its *hine-jez*" and later we'll get
some *I-talyun* food. I request
a *baayg* to carry our bread inside,
but a clerk in Kansas would say *sack*,
and we both giggle at that connotation.
Later, I'll ask if you want to *come with*,
and when I call on your location, I ask
where're you at? You refer to hills
and valleys as *hollows*. On the page
this sounds empty, but from your mouth
it's a yell, and I think because of distance,
how far a voice must travel
over slopes and blue ridges. You laugh
at the plural of you being *yous*, and *eh*
meaning more than just another word
for *huh*. You tell me: *there's only one
way to say kudzu.* I still get it wrong,
stress the *zu* instead of the *kud*.
No, *ya-der-hey* is not in your diction-
ary; is a *whoop'n-a'holler* in mine?
You speak in iambs, naturally,
because it's your mountain culture,
and I speak only when spoken to,
because it's my northern mime.
But there are just as many words
for snow as Appalachian rhyme,
and *hush* and *shush* sound the same
from both our mouths: like brooms
touching dust touching carpets.

Oral History

It's a Sunday in May 2002, and I'm getting prepped
for a free cleaning in a Charlottesville dental office.
I tell the hygienist, the mother of my then-boyfriend,
that my cavities were the result of having braces.
She responds with only, "Open wide. No, wider."

When she fastens the bib around my neck, a lamplight
halo shines through her blond curls. And I think of that scene
in *Little Shop of Horrors* where Steve Martin plays a dentist
and Rick Moranis plays a version of Rick Moranis
(kind and small, with a weakness for lovers who bite).

I know this: that my dental records would be used
to identify me if I'm ever found tied up and tangled
in rhododendron or mountain laurel on the Blue Ridge
Parkway. And I know I would only be lost until I'm found
because of the three amalgam fillings in my upper right molars
and the small chip on my bottom left lateral incisor.

I hope that my breath doesn't smell, as I let this woman
explore my mouth and pick at all my history. I know
she can see my habits: how long I brush, whether I gargle,
whether I floss. Whether I hold my tongue and chew
on my words or practice lip service. Whether I'm good enough.

Her son sits in the corner waiting, fluorided, and perfect.
I grip the vinyl chair as she leans in closer and whispers
into my ear, "Uh-oh, this feels like a soft spot."

Now All Is Echo

but not the goddess, you said, in an argument
we had whose sides I no longer remember.
We were together in a dream and on the side
of a road after noticing a sack moving the grass.
Kittens, it's probably kittens, you said, trying
to scare me in this dream within a dream,
a nightmare, a version of a recurring one. For me
it's always discarded sacks on the road—garbage
bags tied with twine—and inside barely a breath
but still warm, a litter of kittens. The top layer
still capable of mewing. The layers beneath still
and only still. In these dreams, the worst ones,
they live for minutes, enough time to make me think
I can be their savior, at least to one. Those are the worst
dreams. In the versions where we, still together,
pull off the road and the sack is hard, a quarter
full with stiff bodies, the nightmare is less.
There's nothing to do but mourn and praise
the silence, be grateful for the lack of audible
memory. When I save them—take them home,
wrap them in pilled fleece, rub their bellies and beneath
their tails after feeding them, do what their mother
would do—I wake from the dream angry.
Angry at the discarded. The ones who discard.
Angry I wake to no one and nothing but the echo.

Soundtrack for Fall & Forgetting

It's raining and autumn. Outside
everything dark crushes color

with blows of wind and branches.
The perfect setting for a day

inside with wool & wine, and seclusion—
that desired kind.

I've learned the plucks of a banjo
can rhythm the scratch of tree limbs.

A light Béla Fleck—soft haphazardness,
the soundtrack for fall & forgetting.

Only a squirrel—the culprit of a rasping,
a sound closer to pines scraping

house shingles, painted wood siding—
grips the window screen, scuttles

to the pane, back and up, clings
to the mesh with vampirelike claws.

A voyeur wanting in
in the worst way.

I know the act of clinging
has no scent, no sound—it's static,

but still this house reeks of dead fruit: pears
spotted and moldy, fuzzed to their stems.

Is it a law of nature that everything
empty must fill again?

All week, I packed and sealed,
stuffed suits into bags but folded

the towels I'd later unfold, wrap around
my clean arms and shoulders.

A temporary comfort, like wool & merlot
and that myth of solitude.

Revision

This time in my house, I'll bring in the furniture, inside this time
      from the garage.

Years ago, our house—the one we lived in together, thought how cool
      to be new in our twenties with a deed and a driveway,

that house, a brick bungalow with charm—stayed empty for a year
      with bags as dressers, futon for our bed.

That house—hollow without tables and chairs, sofa or stools—
      we didn't know how to fill, except with our voices:

inside the air between rafters and thresholds, all that space,
      we'd loft phrases, pastoral and poetic.

You'd say lines like, *you shed our morning blankets*
      like a dragonfly molting,

and I'd say, *you're wading along the lakeshore, wielding a net.*
      And back and forth, the words we tossed

echoed and faded, bounced in that space we shared
      against emptiness. Maybe if we had created an alcove,

spackled a wall, constructed a partition, or just brought in
      our furniture, we could have secured our words,

trapped them inside, filled our house like an aquarium of language.
      Instead, after coffee that final August morning—

our last together in that house or anywhere, with windows open,
      breeze traveling through—we sat in silence.

The only words were stuck on the refrigerator door. In block
    letters we formed phrases, final and magnetic.

You linked: SHADOWS WE FELL THROUGH
    TRUTHS WE LOST. And I linked: I KNOW

AND MISS A HOUSE A HOME. And all around us, inside
    and quiet, from rafters to thresholds, the wind blew words.

Homecoming

When he came home, he was under
house-arrest and wore a bracelet
on his left ankle. I joked with my sister
about our brother, how he was like a character
in a sci-fi film, and if he ran away,
past the driveway at night, an alarm
would sound, the cops would come, and surely
his ankle would explode like confetti.
We laughed hard at this, not to be cruel,
but maybe just stupid, so young and so full
of late-night movies we captured on cable.
One August night around the fire pit
in our backyard, we soaked corn, dampened
the ears before placing the husks over the fire.
The green hissed then steamed; the coals
popped but didn't escape. When my brother
grabbed a stick and raked the ashes,
I leaned forward and touched his ankle band.
Overhead, loons passed by, reminding us
of our lake, our woods, the goodness
of summer, and all of it ending. Still
we sat on oak stumps cut clean
on each end. Lumberjack furniture.
Yeah, he said, *it's for real but it won't stay*
forever. This piece of jewelry that made him
interesting. Before all this happened,
my brother would never have roasted
corn with his sisters on a clear summer night
when there was so much running to do.

Sugarloaf Mountain, Lake Superior

It seems loaf-like, curved like sourdough
doming at the top. Crags filled with bluebead lily
litter the crest, and the green below, moosewood
and pine, dimples the lake's grin of shoreline.

Below the mountain, not far from here, planted beneath
penny-scented leaves, are ceramic bib-wearing boys
with distended bellies, cherub cheeks, vacant eyes,
and cheeseburgers carried in their arms.

Someone buried them. Buried them thigh-deep,
next to discarded Buicks on copper soil.
In the Big Boy Graveyard, grins and freckles appear
through the trees. And in the woods all around,

would-be Paul Bunyans strut their flannel. They speak
with clipped "ya's" and "eh's," and sneer at the runners
who race the mountain in reflective vests and tractor-tread shoes.
The lake below with its swell, its swallowing deep,

humors only the mountain. Each year the water takes
as its own naive swimmers and freight-ore sailors.
But once, last fall on Sugarloaf's ridge, a bear's heart stopped,
paws mid-climb. A ranger found it there, its coarse fur still bristling.

And the lake below was quiet glass. The wet mirrored the rock.
That water's sapphire sheen, it could have been pride.

If a Bird Frightens a Pregnant Woman, Her Child Will Be Born with a Wing Instead of an Arm

—a superstition about pregnancy

How fortunate Icarus might have been, not needing
    the wax, the collected feathers, not failing and falling
to the heat of the sun. If only his mother, pregnant and craving
    a sunny-side up, had entered a coop of frantic chickens,
if only the rooster had the power to startle bone into wing.
    If only a hen, full and heaving, had squawked to terrify
pores of skin into follicles of down.

How fortunate my brother must be: now he jumps
    mid-winter from heavy fir trees. He climbs up,
flies down past their weighted branches, coasts
    to the bottom, lands with a puff on frozen pine needles,
imprints the snow with his Matryoshka doll frame.
    He does this again and again, without failing, without fear.

How fortunate our mother once craving
    wild berries lost her way while searching the woods.
What luck she was startled by two huge birds, tall blue herons,
    that stabbed the lake water with their long dagger beaks.
When they stretched their wings, so wide and so mighty,
    feathers poked past the oaks and maples. Tips of plumes
brushed against her goose-bumped skin.

First Spring in Suburbia

As if we want to immerse ourselves
        in the whirr and trill of mowers on Saturday,

we open all windows, even the awnings
        sealed since November, to a new discourse:

modern lawn culture. On all sides and up
        the street and block, trimmers and hedgers, blowers

and saws tune conversations of rumbles and ticks,
        hums with motions of margins and gridding.

And when the blue jay pipes in, he interrupts
        with demands to hear his own judgment singing.

That smartass, we say on weekday spring mornings
        early outside with toast and coffee. We'll marvel

at our preference for the squirrel's fat yakking
        at cats and children over the jay's yard sermons.

And when that bird yells and pressures the grackles to group
        in the boughs of maples, that's when

we miss our lake, the sense of loons, the chorus of frogs
        when we lived up north, just last year, just last June.

Now we sigh, hear only as memory those singers so patient
        performing their parts: the loon, the frog,

the wolf, the cricket. This weekend, the jay lectures
     all yards—yells over brawls of motors and sprinklers

as to heedless young students. We listen too. We take notes
     as if somehow we'll catch some reason for seeing it through.

The Bundling Board

was not for sale. And I was free
that night and the next, but listening to you

read antiqued words dusted on plaques in foreplay
shops (boutiques to stroll through while drunk on wine)

was not how I thought the night would end.
I knew we'd take rhythm, apply it

slow—first politeness at wood tables,
over slabs of Gouda, smoked to boldness,

or dollops of Brie. (I liked the way you spread
your rye. You were smooth like that.)

So the optimist in me turned water
into Riesling, drank it too fast, then ordered

some more. You turned seduction
into something quaint—that was new to me,

like a secret talent. Both of us drunk
in consignment shops later, you lectured

on dead owners of Box elm armoires,
copper-bottomed pots, patchwork quilts,

and cast-iron stoves. I lost interest
in vintage gossip, until we discovered

that bed in the corner, all laced and ready
for sleep or sale. The bed frame intact

with old Dutch designs. Everything could be bought
except that wooden plank slicing through the middle,

which kept things clean, which kept the bodies separate.

How after Snowmelt

We checked off our likes, our wants,
and have-nots like items in a suitcase,
like things we'd carry to a weekend
with relatives all grown up. We drove
down a two-lane sided by fields, one
once corn now groomed dirt, the other
black from burning. We compared notes
in the abstract: *what do you think about*
global warming? When you wake to thunder,
do you feel fear, excitement, do you think:
global warming? We repeated ourselves
for comic effect. We laughed at newness:
of spring, of the holding of hands, of simple
robins, and how after snowmelt everything
everywhere smells like excrement.
We turned brave, revealed small truths
about ourselves from observing others
from afar, up close, over years of growing.
I said, *The only people who watch*
Independence Day parades are eight-
year-old girls and white supremacists.
You said, *Those who wear useless accessories—*
scarves in warm weather, belts on tight pants,
watches that don't keep time—were never hugged
as toddlers. For a while, we said nothing.
Our hands rested between seats, between knees,
up on the dash. We kept on driving, wondering
whether we had already gone too far.

Bildungsroman

In 8th-grade biology, our teacher leads us
down the path, takes us through the woods
to learn about chlorophyll and change.

We pass the leaves—the crinkled, the fallen,
whatever remains of green and clinging—
and he lectures on switchgrass instead,

how it hugs the shorelines of ponds and bog thickets.
We study its stems: their shape, their sides
so quick, so capable of slicing.

My hands aren't nimble in the chill of autumn.
The blades, they slip from the tips of my fingers,
and an edge of grass fillets the length of my thumb—

transforms it into a one-gilled minnow.
I wonder at this cut, this slash, this fish lung
gaping at my knuckle. I poke at pinkness:

two folds of skin that refuse to bleed, and I fall
behind the rest of the class, wander alone
among the oak and pine into a moraine.

There I try spooning a fallen elm tree,
one that crashed not long ago.
Now when a breeze pushes its way through,

it bullies only dead branches.
But the sparse hairs on my arms,
how they fray, how they thread.

Cyclic

The odor was septic and made us speechless,
though we'd already lost our voices
when the sun napped dusk, when night's sheet
hushed the traffic, the birds, our thoughts.
It was a peahen hit to the ditch
and decaying. Her left wing shielded
her breast—a draped cape, her final
comfort. The smell of turkey is not
always the same. If we cooked her carcass,
would the scent remind us of arugula,
of berries brined? Of autumn and wood fires,
the late summer's chilled wine? This find,
this bird, we encountered on an evening
that made us question beauty, was she messaging
her last will and flight? Her lofted feathers,
those still sticking to live twigs weighted
with winter berries, led us further still
into the meadow policed by the farmer's
one black horse and one banded cow.
Land we did not own but that owned
our souls in its soil like all life its surface
sends meandering. Not listless in loss,
but lustful for fresh discovery in beauty
found in failed crossings, we crossed
as wayfarers. We foraged through paths
in pastures of sorghum futures and would-be whey.
Our earlobes and nostrils, every follicle
of skin, set as seismographs collecting
fall rot and cyclic decay—any fresh
disturbance—in measurements of awe.

After Reading "A Blessing" by James Wright, I Pay More Attention

to life along the highway. Literal life.
Literal highway. So often I'm consumed
by the dead, the death, the road-kill-carrion
smeared muscle of rodents, raccoons,
and bears. Oh my. Before "A Blessing,"
I noticed not the Guernsey cows,
so golden, so sweet, and the deer
that do their best Baryshnikov
over the ditch. I noticed instead
the porcupine's needles like follicles
from asphalt pores, the fox's tail
bobbing and stuck in a seam of tar,
the feral cats who didn't do their best
Martha Graham to avoid the Honda's tire.
After "A Blessing" and learning about breaking
into flower, and the joy experienced
from observing two ponies nuzzling,
I pay attention. I see turtles living on the edge,
scooping the gravel to lay their eggs.
And my left arm greens to a stem.
I see frogs being improper in the road, right
in the middle of the road, during a rain storm.
And I brush pollen from my shirt.
Those cows, those gentle Guernseys?
I see them, and the fingers on my right hand
become petals. I can't step out of
my body completely and break
into flower, but parts do blossom.
After reading "A Blessing" I'm still
no fool. I can't ignore the sadness of the road,

the literal road, the metaphorical one too.
One morning while running in Madison,
Wisconsin, I saw farther up the street
the shape of a squirrel hovering
over something, some still but soft thing.
I caught up and the squirrel, that visible
squirrel, didn't flee. It didn't leave
its partner, the soft lump in the center
of the road, clearly hit, clearly dead.
This squirrel, this living rodent, this pest
to attics and garages, prodded its dead love.
Nudged her. Wouldn't leave when I ran by,
and only fled to the grove of oaks
when a truck approached. I kept running.
I looked back, and that squirrel
had returned to its partner's side.
That's when I thought I'd break.
That my whole body and heart
would break, but not into blossom.
Instead, I would crumble like a leaf
in November. I would crisp into pieces—
some parts dirt, while others
would sparrow into the wind.

Acknowledgments

Special thanks to the editors of the following publications in which these poems first appeared, some in different versions:

The Ampersand Review: "How after Snowmelt" "The Effigy Mounds"
Anderbo: "Jill Falls for Jack"
Ascent: "Soundtrack for Fall & Forgetting"
Boxcar Poetry Review: "The Bundling Board"
Cimarron Review: "Now All Is Echo"
Crab Creek Review: "If a Bird Frightens a Pregnant Woman, Her Child Will Be Born with a Wing Instead of an Arm"
Decomp Magazine: "Upon Encountering in the Woods, a House with No Driveway, No Trail, No Footpath Leading to the Front Door"
Diagram: "Sky Writing"
Dunes Review: "First Spring in Suburbia"
Failbetter: "Homecoming," "On Learning It's the Midwestern Weather That Makes Us All Crazy"
Green Briar Review: "Upon Learning about Tardigrades from Wikipedia"
Harpur Palate: "First Snow Aubade"
Hawk & Handsaw: "After Reading," "Cyclic," "How Now from Our Front Doorway," "Revision"
The Hopper: "To Skin Bare"
The MacGuffin: "The Awkward Sister's Complaint," "The Day I Lost the Boy to the Girl with Sea-Foam Manners and Wave-Motion Hips," "Sugarloaf Mountain, Lake Superior"
Ocean State Review: "Residence Time"
Opium: "Pharmaceutical"
Pank: "Wresting Heuristics," "Smarch"
The Pedestal Magazine: "Backwoods Colloquial"
Pif Magazine: "To Fell Roaches"
The Quotable: "Waning"

Silk Road Review: "Hunter Orange"

The Southeast Review: "Oral History"

Redactions: Poetry & Poetics: "Of Your Brother Who Left for the War Today," "To Sound Local"

The Texas Observer: "What We Know About Deer Season," "What We Salvaged"

Weave Magazine: "Couch-surfing Upper Michigan after Lincoln, Nebraska"

Written River: A Journal of Eco-poetics: "On Lake Halfsestina"

"Bildungsroman" first appeared in *Prairie Gold: An Anthology of the American Heartland*, eds. Xavier Cavazos, Lance M. Sacknoff, and Stephanie Brook Trout (Ice Cube Press, 2014).

"Residence Time" was reprinted in *New Poetry from the Midwest 2017*, eds. Okla Elliott and Hannah Stephenson (New American Press, 2017).

"Blastomycosis" and "Springs Eternal" first appeared in the chapbook *Residence Time* (Dancing Girl Press, 2016).

"Sky Writing" was featured on *Deep Water*, a poetry series in Maine's *Portland Press Herald*, on February 26, 2017.

"Smarch" was featured on *The 2100 Project* for May 2016.

Many thanks to the following people who helped make this poetry collection possible: Jonas Agee, Grace Bauer, Kelly Cherry, Kwame Dawes, Patricia Emile, Crystal Gibbins, Jackie Harris, Allison Hedge Coke, Austin Hummell, Ted Kooser, Aimee Nezhukumatathil, Naomi Shihab Nye, Christina Olson, and Hilda Raz. Thank you to everyone at the University of Nebraska-Lincoln English Department, Northern

Michigan University English Department, Bread Loaf-Orion Writers' Conference, Sewanee Writers' Conference, and the Hill House Artist Residency.

About the Author

Michelle Menting grew up in northern Wisconsin and Upper Michigan. She is the recipient of awards from Sewanee Writers' Conference, Bread Loaf-Orion Writers' Conference, Crosshatch Center for Art & Ecology Hill House Artist Residency program, Hewnoaks Artist Colony, and the National Park Service Artist-in-Residence program, where she served as poet-in-residence on Isle Royale National Park. An avid trail runner and lake swimmer, she lives in Maine.

www.michellementing.com

www.ingramcontent.com/pod-product-compliance
Lightning Source LLC
Chambersburg PA
CBHW021025120726
47905CB00009B/3191